Falling out of the Skin
into the Soul

Falling out of the Skin into the Soul

A Divan for Scheherazade

Noel Cobb

Godstow Press

First published 2006 by
Godstow Press
60 Godstow Road
Oxford OX2 8NY
Tel. 01865 556215

www.godstowpress.co.uk

ISBN (10-digit) 0-9547367-4-5
ISBN (13-digit) 978-0-9547367-4-3

Cover design by Joanna Migdal and David Smith
Typeset by Jean Desebrock of Alacrity, Banwell Castle
Printed by Hobbs the Printers, Totton, Hants

Godstow Press is conscious of the impact of the publishing industry on the world's
forests and the environment. The paper used for this book is Munken Book Cream,
a wood-free paper that uses no chlorine or optical bleaching agents.

'como irnos cayendo desde la piel al alma'

— Pablo Neruda, 'Solo La Muerte'

for Maria

CONTENTS

BOOK OF THE SINGER

BOOK OF LOVE

BOOK OF GRIEF

BOOK OF OBSERVATIONS

BOOK OF THE SOUL OF THE WORLD

SIX GHAZALS FROM HAFIZ

BOOK *of the*
SINGER

❡ Scheherazade

Beyond the pitiless wastes, northeast of Ghor,
The doorless, ruined minaret of Jám proclaims
The fame of Ghiyas-ad-Din, King of Kings, to the winds.

Don't you love those outrageous tales of things
That never could have happened! Padmasambhava's
Handprints in the rock, Jesus raising Lazarus ...

Orpheus calms the wildest beasts, brings Eurydice back
Alive from Hell. We read of great love between
An Arab and a Jew, a Capulet and Montague.

Only love it's said can reverse all natural laws
Which is why they saw a tortoise fly in Khorasan.
How else could plants bear fruit of jade and lapis lazuli?

Fairytales tell us of lovers who died yet never did.
Some marriages are made in Heaven, some on Earth.
Old Jung said, 'What would our life be without glamour?'

Princess of Stories, Our Lady, child of the Muses,
Rest awhile. The executioner can wait. Pray
Accept this divan to lay your weary head upon.

⁊ The Worn Book

Ghostly dawn mists hang over grey fjord waters.
Our welcome on shore is terse and unsmiling.
We have come from the dark hold and will return there.

If our fingers are numb and icy, even a cup
Of hot coffee is a shout from Heaven.
How glad I was to carry scrap iron from the hold.

Blindly living a walking death, depressed, impulsive,
Careless, indifferent to custom, taking from the Earth
Without paying back, is that what youth is?

The worn book in the young docker's pocket is all he has
Of hope. Words of a poet, dead half a century.
Cries of pain from a man who has lost his love.

Who has told us to stop at the mirror's surface?
Who has taken hold of our arm, pulling us back?
And why do we ignore the hand outstretched?

Who will we see on the other side, but ourselves,
Wondrously looking into each other's brimming eyes?
Ghostly dawn mists hang over the grey fjord waters.

Gift Aid
20 43053748 8024

✗ The Buried Ostrich Egg

How does the migrating bird know when to fly and where?
Dante left his home and country, grieving.
In many dreams I flew and taught my father, too.

Trusting in stubborn stamina and a wide wingspan,
I could fly for weeks without coming down,
Spellbound by the high ideals of lofty loneliness.

The Flying Boy has to land, but what country is his?
Like the President said: 'He is a man without a country!'
Providence designs the pattern of our lives with love.

The bones of cheated Indians wept beneath my bed.
Too many makes of cars have stolen native names.
A country with so many churches has to live in fear.

Old Euripides exiled to Thrace conjured up *The Bacchae.*
Dante wrote the greatest teaching poem since Homer.
Did he miss the nightly roar of lions caged in Florence?

Kneeling in the sand beside his buried ostrich egg
The wrinkled Bushman sighs: 'There is a dream,
Dreaming us'. If we cannot trust the dream, how can we live?

The Gazelle of the Ghazal

Say there is a poetry of praise: Say of the animal,
Moving in time to its own music and distinctive gait
Through the animated cosmos of the poem.

Rilke showed us how the animal of language moves,
Pacing like a panther behind bars or charged with leaps,
But not fired — like the legs of a listening gazelle.

The gazelle of the ghazal leaps to freedom
Through the poem's clearings. Tiresias' daughter learned
To see from her blind father. Cobras kept her company.

Poetry, as Lorca tells us, should not be
'Understandable'. It is an arsenic lobster
Ready to fall on the heads of smug logicians.

Each time a Bushman mother lifts a newborn baby
To the stars, asking them to give it the heart of a star,
Somewhere else a hundred thousand flowers bloom.

The profiteering soul has no enthusiasm for praise,
For extravagance or beauty or delight in Being.
Maybe that is why the nightingales have disappeared.

✗ Honey Dew

Because we love Beauty, her ugly sisters rush
To sit at our table. Jealousy, betrayal, loss
And loneliness eat the food prepared for Her.

An abscessed tooth sent Coleridge to Xanadu.
Did 'dire poison' leave his body more in tune
With the ruinous reverberations of immortal soul?

Naughty, blue-skinned Krishna loves stealing milk.
But if mortals feed on honey dew, what dreams may come?
Boils on his neck, cramps in his gut, Coleridge dreams.

And if a red-haired harpy tries to pluck out your eyes?
Trapped on the crags of Scafell Pike, the poet sees pleasure,
Shame and pain swim through the air like scattered starlings.

What made great Kubla Khan each full August moon
Offer the milk of his snow-white mares
To spirits of the earth and air? Old superstition?

The Poet's nightmare-screams wake the households of his life.
The famed Distributor of Stamps denies him thrice. But can
Grim austerity ever find a passage out of Hell?

Falling out of the Skin into the Soul

Staring into archangelic incandescence,
Andrei Rublev saw burning gold exfoliate:
The shocking flicker of breathing forms.

How many times in free fall through the bardo did you fear
The speed of impact would destroy you? Yet, the sweet
Pandemonium of life was always there to greet you.

When you were sewn into your skin, where was the soul?
Nina Simone, singing *Mr Bojangles* reminds us
Of the Pietà. The soul bears untold years of loss.

Singing all the way from Malaga to the Alhambra
El Tenazas, 'The Tenacious One', arrives, walking.
One lung dead from a knife-fight. A stopped clock of pain.

Does *deep song* come from inscrutable moonlight?
Or is it God who screams? Voice, zigzagging
Like a wounded moth in air perfumed by blood and roses.

It takes a shipwreck to call us back to beauty.
Yes, Pablo, we die in darkness, darkness. Only then
Finally here: falling out of the skin into the soul.

For Jennifer Begg

✄ Schubertiade

Each time the Circle met, night and the mocking
Death-rattle of the streets stepped back.
When Franz played, the wine glasses filled themselves.

Ever known a piano turn into a spinning wheel?
Or, a herd of galloping demons? Or, the West Wind,
Bringing words of longing to Suleika from her lover?

The Circle ceased to know its separate names.
No Schober, no Mayrhofer, no Drei Mädchen,
No Spaun, von Schwind or Vogl, just one pure longing.

That *sehnsucht*, that longing, is what keeps us up all night,
Feverish for one phrase of beauty. One phrase
Is all it takes to make us her willing slaves forever.

Tied to the mast of his own despair, the Captain heard
What his soul rejoiced to hear. Those sounds made all
Who heard them, wild enough to jump into the sea.

When Franzchen died, the Circle still remained. New voices
Found their way into his songs, falteringly at first,
Following the music of his footprints in the snow.

In memory of Eva Loewe

✗ The Coat of Coal Dust

The Ship of Poetry sails on the Sea of Syllables
In love with the entrancing waves of Sapphic dactyls
Hidden in 'perpetual', 'diaphanous', 'voluptuous'.

The drunken boat of poetry shouts with glee
At the martial charges of the trochees, riding
On 'stormtossed whitecaps'. The oars of iambs flash.

Cocooned in his greatcoat, Coleridge composed darting
Over rough ground; Wordsworth, hat and cravat, strolling
Straight paths of raked gravel. But one loved moonlight. Which one?

The coal miner's son began to build his Ship of Death
When he saw his father's shining nakedness emerge
From its coat of coal dust gathered in the pits.

When Enkidu, sick, dreamt a birdheaded man dragged him
To the underworld, Gilgamesh, his friend, cried out:
We must treasure the dream, no matter how terrible!

For one whose name was writ in water, Death itself
Smelled sweet: For, once bending to her open eyes,
He was forever 'mirror'd small in paradise'.

BOOK *of* LOVE

The Swallows of Vallombrosa

When Arthur Miller finally heard the pain
In Marilyn's voice, he said he suddenly knew
The 'inexpressible happiness that tragedy reveals'.

Why do we fear our moment of happiness so much?
Do you remember the swallows of Vallombrosa?
Five brown-capped babies riding high in the boat of their nest.

Crazy idea, to be married in the Palazzo Vecchio
On full-moon day in June. But love longs for excess.
Even the Gods, they say, enjoy the spectacle

Of uncommon human happiness. And we were happy.
Thousands of tiny blossoms in the tall lime trees
Made the streets of Florence a perfumed garden.

Running up the cool stone steps, pink rosebuds in your hair,
Pink satin slippers on your feet, you would have stopped
Botticelli in his tracks, Love's looks so graced your face.

Here, in the City of Flowers near the Arno,
Venus holds Mars in her arms. We kiss and then take hands
What tender, good fortune for this Midsummer Marriage!

Blessing the Marriage of my Brother's Daughter, Sara, to Eric Hachmann

To be touched even once by the mystery of love
Means we can die, knowing what never can die.
The souls of those who are faithful to love

Burn in the brightest of stars in the sky. Here below,
The small band of those called 'Love's Faithful' work
Through the centuries to open the hearts of the Sleepers.

Whom does the Lover see in the face of the Beloved,
But God? What does it matter that the Sleepers say
Love is a dream signalling nothing, a confused delusion?

Love is starlight reborn on Earth, as bread
She breaks with him in the morning, as shining
Grapes he brings to her mouth in the evening.

Morning star, evening star, love rides the wild sea
Of the night, an unsinkable boat, high tides and low.
And whether calm falls, or doesn't, light rises in their eyes.

May he always remember the moonstone of her soul.
May she always remember the fire-opal of his heart.
May this marriage be wine and sweet laughter, a planet of joy.

Waterfalls of Ivy

The swan makes her nest of reeds upon the lake
Behind the willow's curtains. The robin hides
In waterfalls of ivy. The woodpecker carves a cave.

What kind of bird broods on words as if they were eggs?
A word may take years to hatch. Greek myth says the God
Of Love was born from an egg. Is that why Eros has wings?

Eros has wings, but is blind. Meaning he can fly, but sees
With another eye than the 'sensible' one. What Love sees
We cannot know. Until his arrow finds its mark.

But Eros's arrows only serve to ignite a fire.
They do not tend it over time's long years, awake,
Bringing dead wood to keep it alive and burning bright.

Does that mean there is another love, greater
Than the Archer's? A lesser known, a hidden God?
And will he gather the souls of Layla and Majnun

And take them home? And will he teach them how to love
When time dims their eyes and greys their hair and slows
Their pace? Will they finally rest within each others' arms?

❧ The Mazdaen Earth Angel

At night Rodin's lovers leave their marble forms
For Plato's worlds beyond the sky.
But, in the day great joy fills the lover's body.

Everything longs for perfection, even summer, even
Socrates' wife. The Stradivarius longs to release
Bach from the airy frame of its grasshopper body.

God knows why men manufacture violence.
Mothers cry when their babies die, playing with landmines.
But hatred sells, compressed into a metal body.

It was in Ur that the Mazdaen Earth Angel
First spoke to Adam. Now She washes
Radioactive dust from the shepherd's dead body.

Will we soon be able to live without water?
Will a new species evolve where the heart will beat
Without blood coursing through the body?

For years, Rumi, distraught, cried to see God again,
Knocking on doors from Konya to Kurdistan.
Until, spinning, Rumi was Shams and one with Love's Body.

For Robert Beer

❧ The Flight of the Tortoise

Tell me, student, who sits on the throne of your heart?
If no one is there, do not praise emptiness. A heart
Whose throne is empty is a heart as dark as treachery.

In the Caravan of State each camel is loaded
With lies. The President thinks one more will not hurt.
But the camel of good intentions falls and breaks her legs.

The stories of lovers are woven on looms
Made of heartbreak and ruin. Would you buy a ticket
On a boat headed downstream over the falls?

Two things give imagination wings: this wine and your love.
Even the scrabbling tortoise in its heavy shell flew
When love lifted it up off its clumsy legs.

But if Love lifts you up out of yourself, don't talk.
The tortoise only flew because its mouth was shut
Around the stick two flying ducks held in their beaks.

However drunk with You I get, I could not betray
Love's secret. The tortoise only fell from his great height
When he opened his mouth to boast of his delight.

✗ Bluebells

O, soul of soul, what shall I do? I stand outside Her house
All day, singing praises of Her beauty, but She
Will not show Her face for one moment at the window.

Her cruelty is beyond reason. I could cut off
My head for Her as a gift. But She would not accept
My empty skull even as a flower pot.

All Brancusi's calculated craft could not approximate
The polished beauty of a single stone-age hand axe.
We know no more than Kaspar Hauser when we die.

The winter sky says there is nothing to laugh about.
Yes, I know that everything must end in ruin.
Yet, I still persist in planting bluebells in these poems.

In the high sierras of Alpujara friends gather
Around *deep song* in winter. The guitarist listens
Carefully to his singer like a man walking on ice.

Tear open my chest and reach into my heart:
There you'll find the Secret One enthroned.
Noel, with such wealth as this how can you ever want?

⚡ The Evening Primrose

Have you ever heard the evening primrose weep
When the messenger of night arrives? No,
When all the garden falls asleep, she comes awake.

Socrates is the name of that in us which questions
Everything. Yet, underneath everything lies our fate.
If we could but learn to read it, we would awake.

Our lot is the one we chose before birth, remember?
Who is the more unhappy: the one who sees his fate
And goes to meet it, or the one who refuses to awake?

The course of our fate is not only written in the stars.
It is etched into our palms, remembered
By birds flying overhead. The landscape is awake.

Mahler was faithful to his heartache even to the end.
In his Tenth, Salome's siren call is rendered
Senseless by vast doors slamming shut. He was awake.

Have you heard the cries of joy coming from the garden?
It is the evening primrose, throwing wide her arms
To embrace the night, with calm, bright eyes, yet so awake.

BOOK of
GRIEF

⅍ God's Face

I do not want to hear again how captured macaques writhe,
Test-fed drugs through tubes down their throats; how they
Helplessly wring their tiny hands and stare at the sky.

Say you are born as an animal, chances are
You will be used for your meat, your milk, your glands,
Your horns, teeth, tusks, feathers, skin and fur.

The animal-headed Gods of the Upper Nile
Tried to teach us Beauty, Justice, Virtue, Wisdom.
All day the butcher downstairs chops up animals.

How I love the animal-bright look in your eyes!
And when you weep for the animals' pain, I ask myself:
How many lifetimes does it take for the heart to open?

Because Melampous saved the murdered snake's orphans,
They later licked his ears clean, so he could understand
The ancient words of birds and be a healer.

Under the trees a distraught dervish prays: 'O, God,
Show me your Face!' A drunk leans out the Tavern window,
Shouting, 'Have you never noticed the grace of a tiger?'

For Maria

❦ Devotion to the Unborn

For four months of icestorms and winterdark, the Emperor
Penguin waits for his mate to return, holding
The large egg of their unborn chick on his toes.

Clouds sometimes cover the earth, but the stars are patient.
Persephone waits each year all winter, and our mothers
Wait nine months to kiss our baby toes.

How long must the motionless heron wait for a fish?
How long must the Bushman wait for rain?
How many lifetimes did Nijinsky stand on his toes?

When we do not want to wait, the soul grows vicious
In an armour-plated body. The American president
Becomes a giant armadillo with claws for toes.

The generals dream they are computer-guided bombs
Falling from the sky to destroy all trace
Of Humanity's Dark Cradle. No one counts their toes.

Thousands of feet down, Bush's Armageddon bunker
Trembles on springs like an ocean liner or like
The planet shifting in its orbit. A man without toes.

Dali's Giraffe

Inside the heart of the burning giraffe, secrets were kept.
Tiny topaz flagons. Unstoppered and sniffed, the scent
Was divine. 'They've cracked the code for DNA!' Dali jeers.

Why is it when Man tries to be God, he becomes Satan?
Suppose our genes do contain our destiny.
What price will the Fates then exact for our meddling?

What if Jews, Christians, Muslims all are wrong?
What if the one-thousand million galaxies we can count
Are all part of a single living dancer? The All.

Then what? When Plotinus died, a snake slipped into
A hole in the wall beneath his bed. He said: 'Try
To bring back the God in us to the Divine in the All.'

What would the world be without beauty? Imagine it.
Once the hedgerows were alive with rustling wings
And chirrupings. Main streets hosted warblers in their trees.

Am I wrong to grieve for the absence of the sparrow?
Should I be 'philosophical', like my Buddhist friend
Who says, 'All things die. Even this world system will burn.'

✗ Fleeing Balkh

There are so many languages we cannot read.
The big paw prints of the last snow leopard heading
For the peak leave a message in the snow we dare not read.

In North Afghanistan off the road near Balkh
We found domed chambers carved into the hill.
Mahayana meditation caves still two thousand years.

Fearful visions of destruction made Rumi's father flee
With his family. The hordes of Genghis Khan
Razed Balkh soon after. Rumi grew up on the road.

Early exiles to Balkh from Aristotle's Athens
Taught stone carving. That's why Gandhara Buddhas
Look so Greek. Now the Buddhas of Bamiyan are rubble.

Back in England I dreamt the Dharmamudra rainbow cave
High in the Zasker range of Himachal Pradesh
Had been bulldozed. Should we argue with the soul?

There is no God but God, the loud Believers cry.
For every Buddha hacked to bits by fundamentalists
Ten billion synaptic paths are buried in concrete.

Catastrophe

Each Spring, dawn quickens the tempo of the wood doves' call,
And Robert Schumann writes six books of love songs. But what
Is this sadness in the air? Is there an ancient grief

That antedates Man's coming? Are the naked herds
Of elephants unaware of their coming disappearance?
Are great rainforests incapable of tears?

Sometimes it happens that we see ourselves
Caught in the mirror of another's hurt. How many
Times have I admired my wilful image there?

If we are going to be depressed, why not choose something
Really serious to be depressed about? Let's say it,
The selfish soul is always hungry. Then why feed it?

Smaller than an acorn, the hummingbird's heart beats
A thousand times a minute. Drop of rainbow, feathered spark!
You brighten our Book of Hours for a moment and are gone.

No one's death ever stopped the world from turning.
Suppose it did. Everything would collapse. For the Greeks
Catastrophe also meant a plucked string no longer moving.

✗ Searching for Emptiness

Is there a grief hidden in large numbers? Do we weep
When we hear the war budget is twelve billion a month?
Or that this year two million Eritreans will starve to death?

Because we love parades and waving from Rolls Royces,
We split open the heads of whales for precious spermaceti:
Prized lubricant for rockets, watches and fine gearboxes.

When ancient seas shrank with dying whales' screams
Sven Foyn, rich Norse whaler, turned up his oil lamps,
Shouting. 'I thank Thee, O Lord. It is all Thy work!'

The blue whale's heart weighs more than a Red Cross van,
And songs of the Humpback travel underwater for miles.
Nietszche, in his madness, heard them and was comforted.

Long ago a sari-clad sitarist showed me
A carmine-coloured seed. Opening its tiny lid,
She poured out many elephants, small as snowflakes.

What makes a great soul? Would the souls of five hundred
George Bushes go to make up even one Mandela?
Searching for emptiness, the Buddha found only numbers.

The Melancholy Humour

These are the signs: dryness, heaviness, sluggishness,
Lack-lustre eyes, neglect of one's appearance, a mournful
Look. Inwardly, an excess of Saturn and black bile.

There always are two choices: appease the gloomy God
By being more like him, or curb his sway
By calling on the help of Jupiter, the Sun and Venus.

If it suits you, then wear black, visit graveyards,
Stay alone, read Gilgamesh, grow sad with mathematics.
Listen to the sombre drone of Dowland's *Lachrimae.*

Or go outside, away from ugly buildings, on paths
Through leafy oak, near the sound of water. Wear gold,
Hear Mozart, burn aromatic myrrh, smell jasmine.

For softening the melancholy humour, Ficino
Recommends a melt-in-the-mouth made of almonds, sugar
Saffron, cinnamon, pine-nuts and rose-petal syrup.

It's May and cherry blossom time again! And, Oh!
The grateful soul wants to dance among the clouds
Of pink blossom, but for the bodies bleeding in the streets.

BOOK *of*
OBSERVATIONS

Weighing the Soul

'Surely if the soul exists it can be weighed!'
Cried Arthur Koestler, planning to weigh a man at death.
A steel bed was designed to measure change in milligrams.

The man's last breath went out. No weight was lost.
Old Koestler and his wife committed double suicide.
Did no soul suffer then when darkness fell at noon?

But suppose the soul is the savour, the flavour, the taste
Of things: the juice, the rasa of the raga, pressed out
By the winepress of our love for what's beyond us.

Don't you think the grape cries out, 'Spare me! The pressure
Of the winepress feels like death!' Though the vintner answers
'Our art frees Marsyas's soul forever from his skin!'

Each Renaissance has its scheming Joe McCarthy
Stealing the ladder from between the captive soul
In the tower and her selfless lover on the ground.

What weight then made Sandro Botticelli run and throw
His pagan paintings on the flames? If we do not save
The soul, who will? Weightless, it can still be burnt alive.

For James Hillman

✂ Saying No to Alexander

This morning the taste of the air fills the soul with peace.
Wind stops its dancing through the trees. Even the wood-doves
Abandon their insistent incantations of desire.

The secret one reveals herself in moments like this.
The Friend touches your hand and puts a finger on your lips.
For such a moment Hafiz gave all the roses of Shiraz.

After meditating all night on the mysteries of Attis,
The Emperor understands: infinity must be
Restrained. Yet the ghost of Alexander has him by the hair.

Wrapped in a black lion skin, Julian throws open
His tent-flap to the sun. An eagle circles overhead.
Why can't you who knew so much say 'No' to Alexander?

You wrote: 'The greatest of all blessings is reverence
For the Gods.' Yet, you ignored Mars' inauspicious frown.
The Persian campaign falters. All omens say, 'Go home.'

Plotinus taught: 'Turn back toward the One.'
How can philosophy be so misunderstood?
We are all like Julian when we will not turn back.

✗ Listen, Friend

Early I learned that all is not what it seems.
Lesson: stamped gilt letters on a boy's first wallet:
'Genuine imitation synthetic leather'.

The eye of the emerald says: 'I know where God is,
Believe me.' And I did. I trusted stones more than people.
It took me thirty years to forgive my parents.

Without a guide, I would never have found my way
Out of the Dark Wood. Were it not for him
I would still be lost in Hell's murky circles.

Ghalib, you questioned the point of digging in ashes
With the whole body cindered, the heart clearly burnt.
But I'll tell you, that's clearly an assumption.

Huntsman-archer turned to the Dharma through Mila's song,
Black-Hat dancing master, Khamtrul Rinpoche, died
After eight conscious incarnations. How he could laugh!

When the door to the cremation oven was opened.
There lay his heart. Unburnt in the ashes. Listen, Friend,
If you find a teacher like this, don't turn away.

✄ The Train to Rouen

Even as a boy Calvin hated cheerfulness
And sunflowers. In his Geneva, beauty was a crime.
Future artists saw him coming and dove back into the night.

Not Vincent. In Eternity he had already met
Vermeer, Rembrandt, Hiroshige. Already
In the womb he heard sunflowers sing.

For too long the soul has crawled the blind mines, tunnelling
After coal for the ghost of Calvin, eating potatoes
Under a dark lamp. Calvin ate coal by the cartload.

Maybe Calvin's ghost would wither up, if we cut off
An ear and brought it to a brothel. Would old Saturn
Then be satisfied and let us reach high C?

Vincent loved the gold of cornfields, the heat of August sun.
And even though the crows of Calvin kept returning,
There was the ecstasy of Yellow, the Azure of Provence.

What God used you to give us such beauty?
Your work done, you wrote: 'Just as we take a train
To Rouen, we use death to reach a star.'

❧ Ou Allons Nous?

When Gauguin saw the Yellow House in Arles, he knew:
The crazy Dutchman had caught an Inca devil. Leaping,
And squealing, it had bitten him before he could bottle it.

Now everything he touched turned gold! The walls, a chair,
Faces, fields, flowers. Crushed suns! Ground gold!
Gold of the Inca! Vincent was the richest man on Earth!

Gauguin grabbed the imp and swallowed it. The Yellow Christ
Would be chief Inca! Fleeing Arles, he came to Paradise
Where naked innocence strolled barefoot on the beach.

In the end soul summoned all her conjurors: scarlet,
Peach and mauve, cobalt, pink, viridian. Yellow
Found itself outdone. Beauty's the full palette of the One.

Like syphilis, the Christians were destroying Paradise,
Which is *where we're from. What we are* — is greedy.
And *where are we going?* Where do you imagine?

If you do not know the answer, you can at least
Give your life to keeping Beauty breathing in the world.
Learn from Gauguin. He gave his life for that.

℀ Opus III

Sometimes neither right nor left will do. But driving
Straight ahead into a wall? Call that 'crazy wisdom'?
If we refuse to choose, mischief may choose for us.

A great magician in Tibet, you met with mischief
In the West. To your hospital bed I brought Beethoven:
Devotee, through Goethe, of divinely drunk Hafiz.

Ashen-grey and paralysed, you smiled with half your face.
Could you hear Beethoven's tears, splashing on
The open text of Goethe's *Poems of West and East?*

For he could not. He was listening to Schnabel
In '32, tiptoeing through the halls of Heaven,
Playing hide and seek with Hafiz and the angels.

Opus One-Eleven: perfect pianissimo of Life
Evaporating into silence. Where did this music
Come from? Deaf, Ludvig heard the music of the spheres.

Such gifts come from the Skydancers, but there is
Also the wall. Skydancers incline to heretical
Mischievousness. So like Hafiz we must climb the wall.

In memory of Chogyam Trungpa Rinpoche

✗ 'Round Midnight

What is it that happens around midnight?
Is it that our mortal skulls touch the constellations?
Does the true soul emerge from the shadows at midnight?

Where did this frozen eyeball live, what did it see?
Rich US citizens pay well for children's body parts.
Guatemalan street kids rounded up and shot 'round midnight.

Strangers passing Ficino's house near Florence
Stopped, amazed to see light pouring from his study.
Plato and Plotinus discoursed there 'round midnight.

At Duino, searching for the music of meaning
Rilke paced the stormy battlements alone
Crying for help from the angels of midnight.

Nineteen thirty-nine: a noisy room at Mintons. Young Monk
Dreaming of Ruby, fingers the ivory keys
With displaced accents, shaded delays. 'Round midnight.

Staying up all night, all waiting is for sunrise.
But in the dark descent into the loneliness of death,
Does anything mean more than sweet music 'round midnight?

BOOK *of the*
SOUL *of*
the WORLD

✀ Curious Reassurance

The blackbird sings and in its song the world soul sings.
A song without words. A song at dawn for the sun,
Returning. A song at night for the sun's grave going.

Steeped in remotest reverie, the poet marinates
In metaphorical mystery, like the hanks and loops
Of Moroccan yarn boiled in vats of indigo dye.

The schoolboy lies on his back in the grass, in love
With the changing shapes of feminine clouds. Nervous,
Gary Cooper waits for night and breathless Ingrid Bergman.

If there is solitude, if we protect and cherish it,
If there is only time enough, if the crush of life
Does not blot out the blackbird's song, if there is solitude —

Knowing that the gibbons of Sumatra still hoo-hoo
And glide through the tops of vertiginous trees, gives
Curious reassurance to the poet on London Bridge.

The poet listens to the silence in the blackbird's song.
The poet listens even as death everywhere advances.
The blackbird sings and in its song the world soul sings.

For Nicholas Belfrage

Goats' Milk

A mythical man, the teacher, Marcos, hides in the trees
Of Chiapas. Masked riders gallop out of his words
Bringing baskets of fruit and flowers of hope.

Don't forget Fechner's vision: the Earth, an immense
Angel, rolling through space, wreathed in clouds, glorious,
Aware. Our eyes, diamonds among the dewdrops.

Each time one of us dies, an eyelid of the world closes.
After the boy hung himself, everyone remembered
His memories. His desperation, his dreams, now ours.

Because the grass cannot run from the mower
And the rose cannot escape the gardener's shears,
Does that prove that they have no feeling?

The most beautiful taste I have known
Was the taste of goats' milk in a Tuareg camp
Deep in the Hoggar. Desert thorns were the goats' own food.

Where is this poem going? Will its wings carry it
To your heart? There have always been people
Who believed that eloquence kept the world alive.

ℋ Dust

In the hidden temple of the night, the soul speaks:
'So you lost your reputation because you followed me?
Do you think your standing with the One depends on that?

Relax. Accept the dust. It is your proper station.
For the One all things are dust. The world may say
Otherwise, but don't believe a word of it. Believe Hafiz.

This rotten world will press our dust into bricks.
'And great Caesar, dead and turned to clay?' 'Dust into dust.'
'And in between?' 'A glorious illusion. Paradise.

A staggering array of papayas and pianos,
Honeycombs and flying fish! Dancing at the Jade Pavilion!
Springtimes, gold mines, palm trees and sailing ships!

Who could dismiss Love's sweet moment of desire,
Blissfully protected by the trembling roses of the night?
Or the thousand kind and tender gestures of the Friend?

O Noel, however much you fix your thought on ruins
Or on the cruel bewilderment of poverty and war,
You cannot conceal your longing for the One.'

❧ Reckless Extravagance

Dreaming of Danaë one day in Heaven, Zeus became gold.
But three wombs called, not merely one. So God's gold rain
Fell into three. Three boys were born with fists full of gold.

One chose the palette, one chose the bow, one chose language
To play with. Two mothers named their sons 'Pablo'. The other
Named himself. Three God-sons born of that profligate gold.

Nothing could stop Picasso painting. And who could prevent
Neruda taming fireflies in the soul's moonlit jungles?
No one could part Casals from his cello. That was his gold.

It is the nature of the God to inseminate.
Great art is born of reckless extravagance
Married to form. Not wed to fame, the greedy soul's gold.

Before Casals, the Cello Suites were only fugues
Of migratory birds, flightpaths through the dreams of Bach.
Casals' cello gave them baritones rich as pure gold.

Picasso and Neruda too worked gold for the people.
Pablo Casals. Pablo Picasso. Pablo Neruda.
Three Pablos fathered by a God become gold.

For Kevin Coates

Looking for Salt

All day I have been thinking of the sadness
In the eyes of large animals. They stare at us so.
Have you ever looked into a blue whale's eye?

What if even trees and stones were watching us?
But an eye has two uses: to see through and to weep with.
Something blind in the zygote wants to create an eye.

Outrageous defiance. The matador kneels, his back
To the bull. Spellbound, Picasso is all eyes.
We know how he envied Rembrandt's 'old elephant eye'.

Suppose the fool and the wise man each exchanged
An eye. Would this make a wise man of the fool?
The Buddha taught that sight exists *before* the eye.

All night, elephants walk through my house, swinging
Their trunks, looking for salt. Each elephant is a child
Of divine Memory. Centuries of love live in each eye.

At ninety, Picasso would still not give up and die.
His celestial twin, the Harlequin, trance-dances
In a galaxy of flowers. And each flower is an eye.

For Mark Rylance

✗ Why Rumi Stayed Awake

Before the rain the night is full of listening.
Each rose bush a giant ear, listening
To the sighs of a hundred thousand sleepers.

The breathing of the world asleep is such music
To the rose. The noises of the day destroy
The rose's pleasure hearing raindrops forming far away.

To be awake when all else is sleeping
Was Rumi's great desire. With the ears of the rose bush
He heard the dreams of the wood dove and the robin.

A ball of bones and bright feathers holds a whole world.
The robin hops on legs thin as straws.
Without love, who would wish to exist?

What does the robin dream? What do men and women
Dream? Who cares what robins dream, except the poet?
When Rumi stayed awake all night, it was because of love.

There are those who say that after death there is nothing.
Tell that to the rose bush and hear her gentle laughter:
'Some people sleep so deep they lose all sense of dreaming.'

For Robert and Ruth Bly

The Clover's Breath

Someone in us is suspicious of our desire to be
Generous. We have signed up with the Merchants of Greed.
Colourful ads warn us not to give to the poor.

Because his paintings hang so quietly
On the plush gallery walls, we search for any trace
Of negligence in Vermeer's household books.

The sun sheds its light on even the darkest moon
And rain falls without ever asking for pay. Unabashed,
The Zebra nakedly displays its exuberant art.

Unpleasant things appear when we think we have won.
So many shadows creep into the poem before we reach
The end. Right now large numbers are ramming the door.

Hooked and tangled in the nylon lines of arctic trawlers
One hundred thousand albatross are killed each year.
The Ancient Mariner killed one and disaster struck.

Still, we trust the Worker Bees of the World to return
Laden with praise from the sweet mouths of clover.
The clover's sweet breath is its gift to us all.

For Allan Madsen

SIX GHAZALS
from HAFIZ

✗ Enough is Enough

One rose from the world's garden is enough. Under
The open sky, the shady fountain of a cypress
Is enough. Of weighty things a full cup is enough.

God preserve me from associating with hypocrites.
They say good deeds lead to the palace of paradise, but
A room in the Master's hermitage is enough.

Sitting on the river bank, watching life pass by,
Watching pain or money change hands in the bazaar,
May not be enough for you, but for us it is enough.

The Friend is here among us. Why look further?
I'm knocking at your door. For God's sake, don't send me
To heaven. Just to lie by your gate is enough.

Let me see you just one moment on the day I die,
Then take me, unchained and free, to my grave.
This intimacy with the Friend is more than enough.

Hafiz, it is wrong to complain about the source
Of your fate. There is a nature which flows like water
And there are ghazals which flow likewise. That is enough.

✄ Who was She?

If we had only tasted a drop
From her rose-petal lips. But she left.
We could not gaze at her enough. And she left.

Perhaps she found us tiresome. She packed
Her bags. We could not even catch up with her dust,
She rode so fast. We fell behind. She left.

We said all the magical spells we knew.
We chanted mantras and mystic prayers
To bring her back. But she had really left.

Her burning look ignited fires of devotion.
We were undone. It was clear
To anyone what we had paid for that glance. She left.

Wrapped in dappled light, she strolled among the rose trees
Perfuming the Garden. This was the place of union.
But we didn't go to meet her there and she left.

All night long we groaned with weeping.
Just like Hafiz. Because, God help us,
We were too late to say goodbye ... she had left.

The Sun's Blazing Tavern

Happy the day I leave this ruin. Where may the soul
Find rest? Where is my love? Though your road
Leads nowhere, I'll still follow the trace of your scent.

Though my heart is sick and my body decaying,
I can still move quick and fresh as the wind at dawn
To worship the sight of your cypress-like stance.

Estranged from you, this prison, although
In dearest Isfahan itself, is still a prison.
I'm clearing out. I'll go to Solomon's realm.

I'll travel this road on my head, like a pen,
To be with you. My heart, a split nib, will weep
Blood to write the lines of my ghazals.

I promise that if this grief ever leaves, I will
Go to the door of the Sun's blazing tavern, dancing
And singing your glory like any speck of dust.

Free spirits do not suffer the pain of those
Who are cruelly burdened. Oh, you saints,
Give me the grace and ease of inhuman endurance.

✗ What Place Sleep?

On the one hand, you have the Righteous One
On the other, you have dissolute me.
Do you see how far it is from one to the other?

What have piety and righteousness to do
With the madman's path? There,
The drone of the sermon. Here the rabab's wail.

I am sick to death of systems, the hypocrite's garb.
Where is the Master hidden? Where is pure wine?
Where is that loving look? Where the reproach?

What did the enemy see in my love's face?
On the one hand, a dead lamp. On the other,
A candle of the sun.

Don't be seduced by the dimple in her chin:
In that road there is a deep well dug.
Oh heart, where are you going in such a hurry?

Listen, friend, do not covet rest and relaxation
From Hafiz. Can you tell me what rest is? Or
Which way, patience? And where, what place sleep?

❧ Without that Longing

In the factories of the atom there is nothing
Fashioned by the universe which alone exists.
So, wine-bearer, fill our glasses! All this is nothing.

If you do not long to be in the arms of the Beloved,
What does it matter that you speak of the heart, or sing
Of soul? Without that longing, soul is nothing.

Why go around feeling indebted to Heaven's Trees
For their shade, when, after one glass of this wine,
Those great cypresses dissolve into nothing?

A few hours' rest in this mirage-oasis are all
We have, on each side surrounded by the desert's vast jaws.
So, wine-bearer, more wine! For time is nothing.

Just because you call yourself 'spiritual' and practise
Piety and discipline, don't think you can hide
In smugness. Such zeal is a sham and is nothing.

Hafiz, for some, your name may be distinguished,
But among the drunken madmen of the tavern,
Distinctions of 'better' or 'worse' mean nothing.

✗ To Reach the Heart

These days, oh my heart, the only impeccable
Companions left are a glass of this wine
And a book of good ghazals.

You'll have to go alone, the passage to freedom
Is narrow. Raise your glass. Do you think
There is an alternative to this sweet life?

I'm not the only one in the world
Absolutely paralysed with laziness. Even
Great spiritual Knowers don't use what they know.

Anyone travelling this road of pain
And pandemonium who has any sense
Can see that this world is a worthless trick.

How my heart has longed for a glimpse
Of your face. But everywhere death
Leaps out of the crowd to mock my hopes.

Love's tresses may be chains that bind, but never mind.
Hold on tight and stop saying
Good luck and bad come from Venus and Saturn.

Hafiz is so drunk with the wine of pre-eternity
That no time will ever find him sober. Yet see, he
Is the one whom the Master has summoned.

AUTHOR'S NOTE

i

Three things immediately attracted me to the poetic form of the ghazal: its potential for grace and for beauty combined, in the best examples, with unexpected leaps of imagination – exhibited in sudden and subtle changes of direction in image and existential terrain.

The ghazal originated in Persia (modern Iran) around the tenth century, arriving in India by the twelfth. The word *ghazal* literally means 'a conversation with the beloved', making it essentially a love poem – where the beloved might be a mortal human being or the divinity itself, or even both. At times the ghazal expresses the passionate longing for union in the absence of the beloved, but it can also tell of the melting dissolution of self when the beloved is present. In the hands of different masters the ghazal becomes expressive of different moods: from melancholy to ecstatic, from whimsy to anguish.

The ghazal is such an extraordinary poetic form; and in English we can hardly reach the heights to which masters like Rumi and Hafiz took it. But that is no reason not to try. Many of the present poems were written in the darkness of the night or in pre-dawn light when everything is still. The great ghazals of the past seem to be born out of this stillness. When we listen to this silence, we can just about make out the angelic voices that spoke or sung to Hafiz and Rumi. This is the time-out-of-time when the soul speaks to the spirit and the spirit bends to hear it. In such ghazals as wide a range of emotions as possible is allowed – not simply the usual emotions one expects to find. This is mirrored in the number and diversity of animals which appear in the poems. They carry the real emotion and show the way.

ii

There is much grief in this collection – for us human beings, and for our fellow species on the planet as well. These ghazals were born out of the realization that western 'civilisation' has neglected our interwovenness with the Soul of the World for far too long; something I must thank James Hillman for calling to my attention in the early 1980s. Many of these poems have their origins in the time of the build-up to war in Iraq – in conversations in London with the American poet Robert Bly, there to read his translations of Hafiz to a largely Persian gathering.

It was then that, studying Bly's own masterful examples, I began working with the adapted form of the ghazal he had devised. You see, in Persian a ghazal consists of a sequence of couplets (called shers). Each sher should be a complete, detachable poem in itself and must end if at all possible with a full stop. The tradition is that one can leap from one 'world' to another with each successive sher. Therefore one sher might be a miniature love poem, the next could be a philosophical idea, the next a lament or perhaps an intimate confession. The possibilities of leaping give the ghazal its mysterious and often cryptic atmosphere, because the poet might choose not to reveal the real subject of the poem.

iii

The traditional ghazal is made up of between five and fifteen *shers* – where the total number of syllables in each *sher* can be anything between twenty four to thirty six. Couplets *(shers)* of thirty-six syllables make very long, eighteen-syllable lines. I agree with Bly that this line-length in English is unwieldy and unworkable, and have followed his brilliant invention of a form for the ghazal in English which makes each *sher* consist of *three* lines, with a total number of syllables in each stanza (or English *sher*) of thirty-six (plus or minus three). Though this is not as strict as in the classic Persian form, it feels right for the nascent emergence of the 'English ghazal'.

Beyond these conventions we should be aware that, in the classical ghazal, the poet would usually employ the radif – a single word repeated in a set pattern throughout the poem. For example, a word used once or twice in the first line of the poem is then repeated as the last word of each sher. I have succeeded in doing this in only a small number of ghazals, but I feel that we must not dismiss this aspect of the form. It would be like sitting down to weave a Persian carpet and dropping the intricate repetition of tiny motifs that occur in those matchless designs from Konya, where deep secrets are embedded in the background forms of the lozenges. Finally, I note that the last sher of a ghazal traditionally contains a reference to the poet and speaks to him personally. As a rule, I have not always followed this custom, and purists may find this a fault.

iv

Some Sufis would say that ghazals are written only for intelligent people, and what that means is that the reader must not only enjoy the sense of excitement that comes from the ghazal's wide ranging images and ideas but be prepared to stay with the poem until it begins to glow from one's own participation and the opening of one's heart.

I have therefore allowed myself the widest circumference in drawing upon cultural, historical and theological references. Thus, you will find Vermeer mentioned in a poem along with zebras, clover and generosity. Or Picasso, brought in along with elephants, divine memory and the Harlequin.

These poems came to me on the vast aromatic winds blowing out of Anima Mundi. But primarily they are brought to life by the warming breath of the beloved. Their purpose will be complete if they encourage a longing for 'divine conversation' (sohbet) in those who resonate to their music.

v

The source of the idea to gather the ghazals into smaller sections, called 'Books', arose from my discovery of Johann Wolfgang Von Goethe's *West-Eastern Divan* of 1819. Entitled the *West-Österlicher Divan* in German, it has been called his greatest cycle of poems and, along with his *Faust*, his most important and personal work – ranging in content from passionate love lyrics to reflective poems commenting on the wars and horrors of the world of his time.

The word *divan* comes from the Middle East where it originally referred to the cushions on which a ruler's advisory counsellors would sit. From there it became a word denoting an assembly or collection, which in turn led, in Arabic, Persian and Turkish, to using the word to refer to 'an anthology of poems'. All these senses often combine in traditional titles of collections in those languages. Goethe's model was the Divan of Mohammed Shams-uddin Hafiz of which the first complete translation from the Persian into a European language was into German in the early part of the nineteenth century. This translation inspired Goethe to begin his own West-Eastern Divan in 1814.

Just as Goethe divided his Divan into sections, called Book of the Singer, Book of Hafiz, Book of Love, Book of Observations, Book of Displeasure and so on, I have repeated this idea, though with fewer books. At a future time, I hope to enlarge this Divan with other poems, in which the themes will range even more widely than at present, so aiming to mirror Goethe's wonderful example of diversity.

Goethe's poems are, with few exceptions, not translations of Hafiz, but original outpourings from a man so inspired by the 14th century Persian poet that he seems to have felt himself to be a 'spiritual twin' or reincarnation of the earlier one. Goethe, as many after him have claimed, said that as a poet Hafiz 'cannot be equalled.' But to attempt to discriminate between the greatness of Rumi (1207-1273) and Hafiz (1320-1389?) is as hopeless as trying to judge which of two brilliant stars in the night sky is the more magnificent.*

What can be said about Hafiz …?

Persians (Iranians in today's world) have revered Hafiz so much that it has become a national custom when in doubt about a course of action to take the poems of Hafiz from the book-

---

* A note on my 'versions' of ghazals from Hafiz's Divan: I have reworked a small number of Hafiz's ghazals in English translations – feeling my way toward a rendition which seemed 'truer' than what I found in existing translations. This may seem impudent and irresponsible to those who feel that I have no right doing this, as I do not speak Persian. I can only offer in my defence that I felt moved by the spirit of the great poet to do this and perhaps these 'versions' come closer at times than the existing 'translations'.

shelf and open them at random, finding an answer to their question in the lines they first see – much as we today do by consulting the hexagrams of the I-Ching.

I'll never forget the first lines of Hafiz I heard from Robert Bly, who had in fact translated them:

> *The Sultan of Pre-Eternity gave us this casket of love's grief*
> *as a gift:*
> *Therefore we have turned our sorrow toward this dilapidated*
> *travellers' inn we call 'the world'.*

I'll also never forget hearing Bly sing the following Sufi 'mantra' from Hafiz, one day in 1995 when we were walking the cobbled streets near the castle in Cesky Krumlov in Bohemia. From this you can see how Hafiz challenged the conventional mind.

> *Let's take the yellow flowers*
> *And throw them in the air!*
> *Let's pour the wine*
> *The best that can be found!*
> *Let's break the bowl*
> *Of the great Heaven*
> *And start the Creation*
> *Over again!*

To be even so bold as to mention one's name in connection with Hafiz could be seen as high poetical hubris, but I invoke him out of great love and admiration, with no intention that I should stand on the same plane. There is one poet living, however, who can and should be, mentioned in the same breath as that great master, and that is Robert Bly. So much of what I have learned about images and imagination in poetry, I have learned from that great poet. And that only touches the surface of the depth of my gratitude. His own ghazals, in the collection The Night Abraham Called to the Stars, are the finest contemporary poems I know.

GODSTOW PRESS

*Because philosophy arises from awe, a philosopher is bound
in his way to be a lover of myths and poetic fables. Poets
and philosophers are alike in being big with wonder.*
ST THOMAS AQUINAS

THE SONG OF ORPHEUS, the music that charms stones,
wild animals and even the King of Hades, is the song of
poets who have a sense of the divine at heart. For the
forces of greed and evil to succeed, that song must be
drowned out by noise.

What is today if not noisy? Not only in our society but
within ourselves there is the clamour of many distractions.
Just living life we forget ourselves and the song that we
heard as children is heard but rarely if at all.

The aim of Godstow Press is to sing the Orphic song,
through books of fiction, poetry and non-fiction, as well
as through CDs. Besides publishing first editions we
shall include on our list works which have been privately
produced by writers and musicians who have thought,
perhaps, that they sing alone.

Together, artist and audience, we shall form a choir.

If you would like to be on our mailing list, please get
in touch with us.

Godstow Press
60 Godstow Road
Wolvercote
Oxford
OX2 8NY
UK

www.godstowpress.co.uk

info@godstowpress.co.uk

tel +44 (0)1865 556215